SMART BRAIN RIGHT BRAIN

An Introduction to Physical Sciences

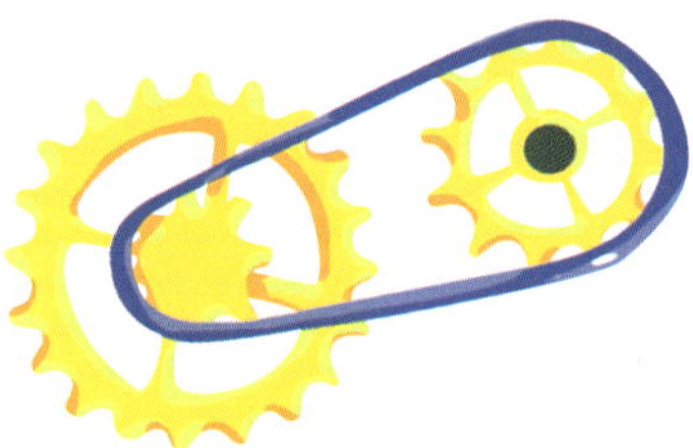

Om KIDZ
An imprint of Om Books International

Om Kidz | Om Books International

Reprinted in 2023

Corporate & Editorial Office
A-12, Sector 64, Noida 201 301
Uttar Pradesh, India
Phone: +91 120 477 4100
Email: editorial@ombooks.com
Website: www.ombooksinternational.com

Sales Office
107, Ansari Road, Darya Ganj
New Delhi 110 002, India
Phone: +91 11 4000 9000
Email: sales@ombooks.com

Author: Shweta Sinha
Editor: Kirti Pathak
Art & Design: Anshuman Pandey, Gaurav Bhandari, Harish Arya

ISBN: 978-93-5276-833-2

Printed in India

10 9 8 7 6 5 4 3 2

CONTENTS

1. Simple Machines

Dana's mother is helping her cut out paper flowers for a school project. Which of these methods should she use?

1. Tear out by hand.
2. Use scissors.

If Dana's mother chooses scissors, her work becomes easy. She can cut the flowers neatly and faster.

You are at a grocery store with your parents. How will you carry the provisions you buy at the store?

You have two options:

1. Carry the stuff in your hands everywhere you go.
2. Put it in a shopping cart and wheel it around the store.

Surely, the cart is a better option.

The scissors and the cart - both are machines. A machine is a tool that makes our work easier and faster.

POCKET FACT

Since time immemorial, humans have been using machines to make their work simpler and easier.

Machines come in many forms, shapes and sizes. An instrument with few or no moving parts is called a **Simple Machine**. There are six types of simple machines - Wheel and Axle, Wedge, Screw, Inclined Plane, Lever and Pulley.

Wheel and Axle

What is common between your bike, a car, and a bus?

1. These machines help us travel.
2. They all run on wheels.

Wheels rotate around a rod called an **axle**. Original wheels were simply tree branches cut into a round shape. They were invented in Mesopotamia. Today we use wheels made with metal and rubber.

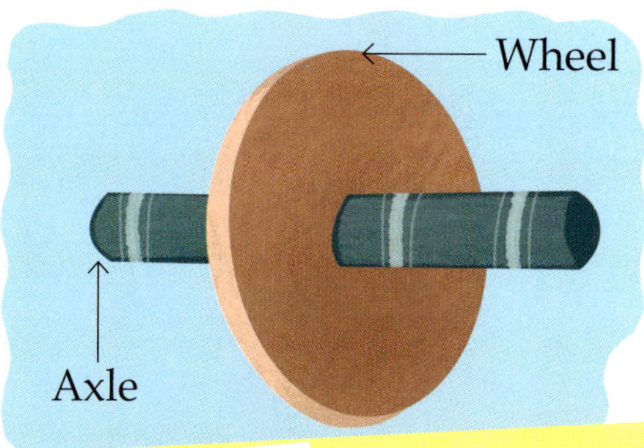

POCKET FACT

A Complex Machine uses one or more simple machines to work. A car is a complex machine because it is composed of several simple machines.

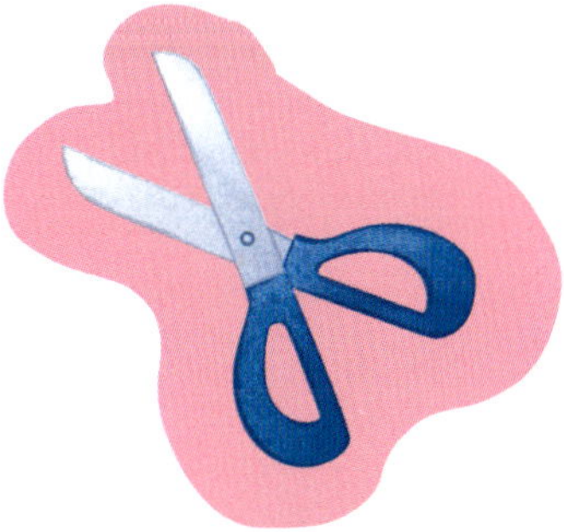

Wedge

How do scissors cut paper? Or a knife slice vegetables?

They have a thin, sharp edge to do the job. This is a **Wedge**.

A wedge is thin at one end and thick at the other. It helps to break things into small pieces, keep things apart and hold an object in place.

The first wedge was probably made nearly 2.6 million years ago.

DID YOU KNOW?

Your mouth is full of wedges. These are your teeth.

Screw

A **Screw** is a thin, pointed piece of metal. It is another common simple machine we use everywhere.

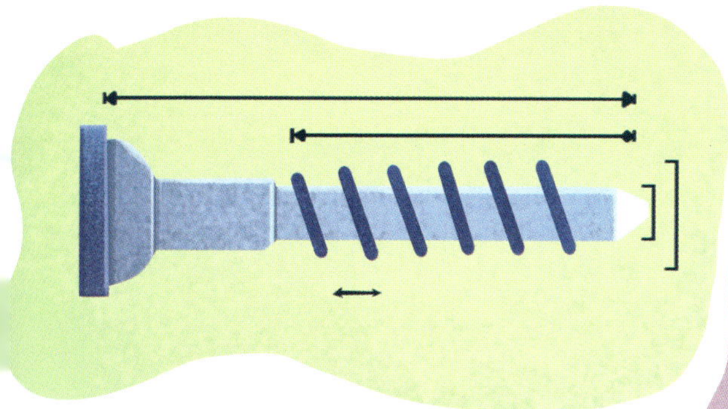

We use screws to join things together. Pieces of a toy car are fastened together with screws. Screws are used to fix handles on doors or to hang pictures on walls, etc.

Look around your house and find as many screws as you can.

DID YOU KNOW?

The invention of a screw was done to extract oil from olives!

Inclined Plane

Suppose you have to keep a heavy box on a high shelf. How would you do it? Throw the box up and pray it lands on the shelf without crashing down?

Not a cool idea. A better way is to push the box up an **Inclined Plane**.

An inclined plane is a flat surface that connects a lower level to a higher level. Staircases, ramps and escalators are examples of inclined planes.

DID YOU KNOW?

Egyptians used inclined planes to build pyramids. Ramps helped them carry stones to the top.

Lever

A **Lever** makes lifting weights easier. It is a board or a bar that rotates on a turning point.

A seesaw is a lever, where a flat board rests at the centre. When you sit at one end, your friend sitting at the other end is lifted up.

Activity: Make a simple lever

Rest a ruler on a building block. At one end, place a heavy object, for example, a battery. This end is lowered because of the weight of the battery.

Now press on the raised end. You are able to lift the end with the battery with just one finger.

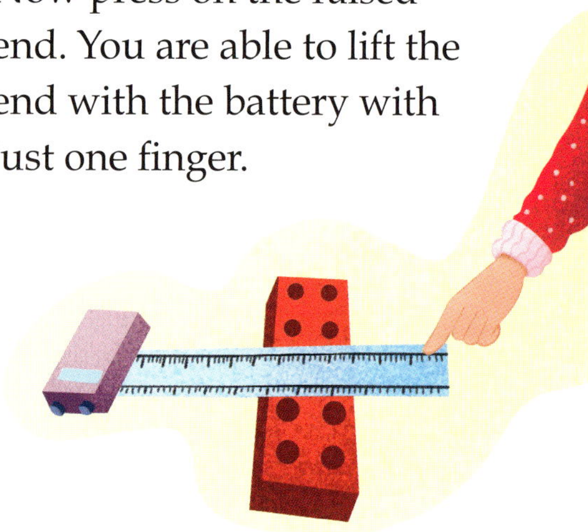

POCKET FACT

Bottle openers, fishing rods, tweezers and crowbars—all use levers.

Pulley

To lift an object up, you pull it down. Sounds strange, doesn't it? But this is exactly what a **Pulley** does.

A pulley uses a rope over something round, usually a wheel. A flagpole has a pulley.

Make a simple pulley by hanging a rope or a ribbon over a door knob. On one end, tie a book. Now pull the free end of the rope down. The book rises with the rope at the other end.

DID YOU KNOW?

The Greek scientist, Archimedes, was the first one to come up with the idea of Simple Machines.

2. Motion

In a playground:

The swing goes back and forth.

The seesaw goes up and down.

The merry-go-round goes round and round.

POCKET FACT

We cannot imagine a world without Motion. Even the Earth keeps moving around the Sun.

In a playground, we may also see children playing and running around; going down the slide behind each other; someone tossing a frisbee in the air; a dog rolling on the grass nearby.

What is Motion?

All the movements that you see are **Motion**.

When you walk to school, you are in motion.

When a car moves, it is in motion.

POCKET FACT

Position is where an object is at any given point in time. Motion is a change of Position.

Some types of Motion are:

- Throwing
- Swinging
- Sliding
- Rolling
- Jumping
- Spinning
- Zigzagging

Can you think of more types of motion?

POCKET FACT

The speed with which an object moves in one direction is called Velocity.

What affects Motion?

Can something start moving on its own?

No. To change the position of an object, motion needs **Force**.

A cart moves only when you push it.

A box moves only when you lift or push it.

A ball moves only when you kick or throw it.

POCKET FACT

An object will remain stationary until a force makes it move. Force and Motion go hand in hand.

Each motion takes place with a varying **Speed**.

A swing remains still until you push it. If you push it gently, the swing goes slow. If you push it hard, it goes fast.

What did you do to increase the speed of the swing?

You pushed it with a greater Force.

DID YOU KNOW?

An astronaut can leave a tool in space and the tool will remain in the same spot as there is no force to move it.

3. Force

How do you open a closed door? You push or pull it open.

How do you put away your books and toys scattered in the room? You lift them to the cupboard.

How do you move a frisbee? You simply throw it.

To move anything, you need **Force**.

Pushing, pulling, lifting and throwing are all forces.

Force is the strength or energy that moves something.

What can Force do?

How do you stop a moving ball?

You catch it with your hands. You 'pushed' against the ball's motion to stop it.

In tennis, players use racquets to hit the ball back and forth.

They use force to change the direction of the ball.

POCKET FACT

You need more force to stop a ball moving at a faster speed.

A force can make an object go from standing still or moving slowly to moving quickly. This increase in speed is called **Acceleration**. Force can also make objects slow down.

DID YOU KNOW?

When you walk on snow, your feet apply pressure and footprints are formed. Pressure is a type of force.

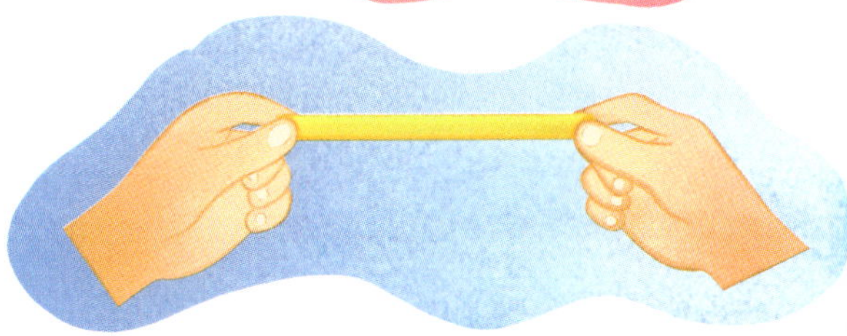

Force also changes the shape of objects.

Try it yourself:

Squeeze a plastic bottle. What happened?

The shape of the bottle changed.

Stretch an elastic band. Take a lump of play dough and squeeze it. Crush a piece of waste paper. Bend a stick.

What do you see?

You changed the shape of the objects by applying a force.

4. Friction and Gravity

We are surrounded by various forces all the time. They run the world.

What happens when you push a toy car across the floor? Does it keep moving at the same speed? Not really. The car slows down and stops after a while.

The force that slowed down the car is **Friction**. Friction occurs when two objects rub against each other. The toy's wheels rubbing against the floor creates friction.

DID YOU KNOW?

It is because of friction that we walk without slipping. When we walk, our feet rub against the floor and create friction.

POCKET FACT

Gravity gives us weight. The bigger our size, the greater is the Earth's pull on our body.

Gravity is another force that is always around us. Ever wondered why things always fall down? Sir Isaac Newton did, when an apple fell on his head. He discovered that the Earth always pulls things towards it.

The force with which the Earth pulls us is called Gravity. This is why our feet remain on Earth and we do not fly off into space. Skydivers begin to freefall before parachuting to a landing because they are pulled by the force of gravity.

5. Magnet

Magnetism is one of the most useful forces in nature. We use it to run motors, generators and even high-speed trains.

There is a story about a shepherd named Magnes in ancient Greece whose shoe nails got stuck to a rock containing a mineral called magnetite. This is how the first magnet was discovered. Have you seen a **Magnet**? Do you have any fridge magnets at home?

Take a magnet close to your refrigerator. The magnet almost gets pulled away from your hand.

Bring it close to a board pin and the board pin sticks to the magnet. Aren't magnets the coolest things in the world?

POCKET FACT

Hitting a magnet with a hammer or heating it will make the magnet lose its magnetism.

DID YOU KNOW? You can magnetise an iron nail by rubbing a magnet on it for a little while.

Try this:

Take the magnet close to a pencil. Did anything happen? No, the pencil did not move.

Take the magnet close to a plastic toy. Even the toy does not move.

Magnets only attract certain metals including iron, cobalt and nickel.

Poles of a Magnet

All magnets have two ends, called **poles**. One end is the north pole, while the other is the south pole.

When two magnets are close to each other, their opposite poles attract. This means that the north pole of one will stick to the south pole of the other.

If you bring the same poles together, the magnets repel.

All magnets have poles regardless of whether they are shaped like a bar, a ring or a horseshoe.

DID YOU KNOW?

Even if you cut a magnet in half, it will still have a north pole and a south pole.

Our Earth is one big bar magnet. It has the North Pole and the South Pole and it interacts with other magnets too.

Place a bar magnet on a flat surface. See how it spins around to point its north pole towards the north direction. Earth's magnetic field attracts the magnet and makes it spin.

This behaviour of magnets is used in a **Compass**. A compass is a tool that tells directions. It has a magnetic pointer that always points northwards.

POCKET FACT

Since the Earth's North Pole attracts the north pole of a magnet, the North Pole should technically be called the 'South Pole'.

Match the following Motions:

swing

jump

bend

throw

skip

stretch

Simple Machines

Look at the pictures. Write the name of the simple machine that they represent:

lever	wheel and axle	wedge
inclined plane	pulley	screw

(a)

....

(b)

....

(c)

....

(d)

....

(e)

....

(f)

....

Machines and their moving parts

Mark **Yes** on the machine that has moving parts and **No** on the machine with no moving parts.

(a)

Yes

No

(b)

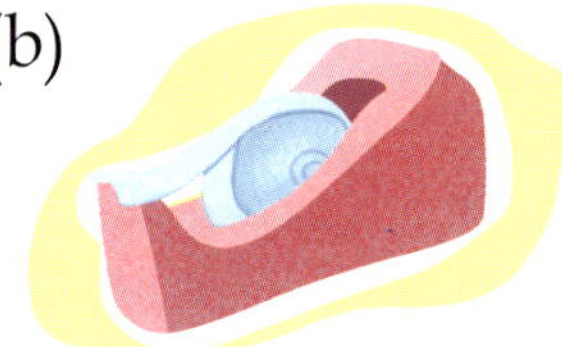

Yes

No

(c)

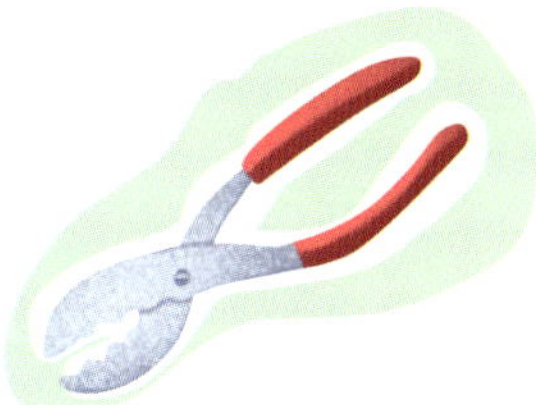

Yes

No

(d)

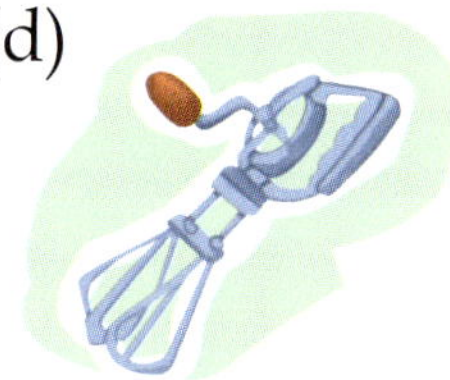

Yes

No

(e)

Yes

No

(f)

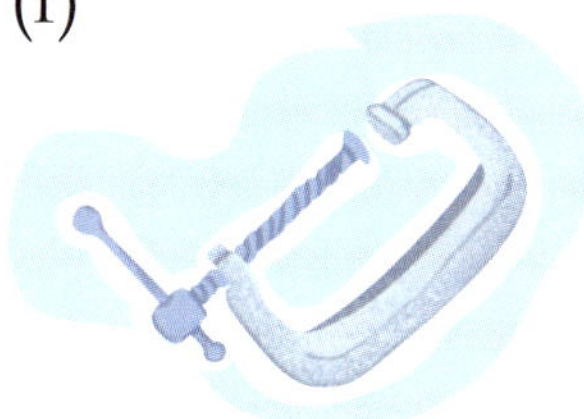

Yes

No

Magnetic Attraction

Tell whether each pair of magnets will attract or repel.

(a)

attract repel

(b)

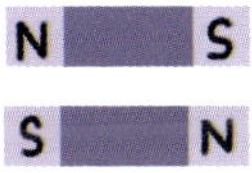

attract repel

(c)

attract repel

(d)

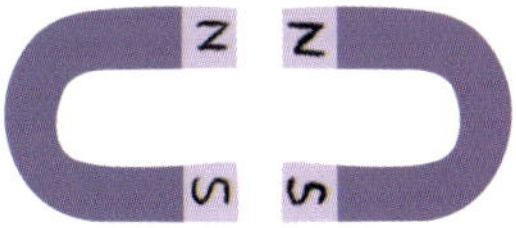

attract repel

(e)

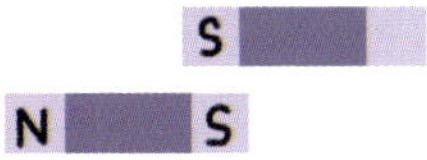

attract repel

(f)

attract repel

(g)

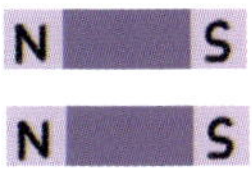

attract repel

(h)

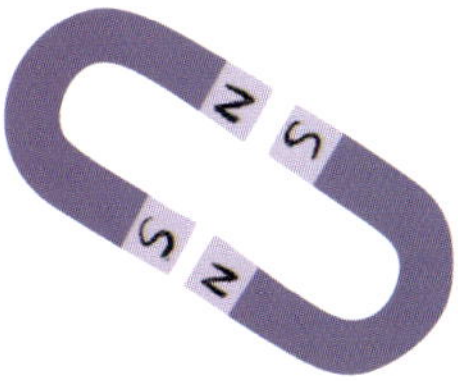

attract repel

(i)

attract repel

GLOSSARY

Attract	to get pulled towards
Compass	an instrument to tell directions
Crowbar	a steel bar used to pry open or loosen
Energy	power that makes things work and move
Escalator	a moving staircase
Extract	to pull, or draw out with special skills
Instrument	a mechanical tool
Machine	a device that modifies force or motion to do some work
Magnet	a piece of metal that attracts certain types of metal towards itself
Motion	a change in position or location
Repel	opposite of attract; to back away
Screw driver	a hand tool for turning a screw

ANSWERS

Page 28.

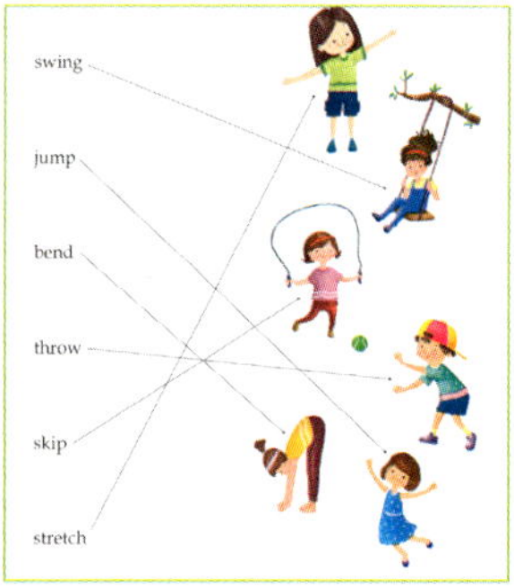

Page 29. (a) pulley (b) wheel and axle
(c) lever (d) screw
(e)wedge (f) inclined plane

Page 30. (a) No (b) Yes
(c) Yes (d) Yes
(e) No (f) Yes

Page 31. (a) repel (b) attract
(c) attract (d) repel
(e) repel (f) repel
(g) repel (h) attract
(i) repel